Born of the Spirit

By
Kathleen Claussen

Cover photo is by author's son;
artwork is by author's grandsons at ages 8 and 5.

"Not to us, O Lord, not to us
but to Your Name be the glory
because of Your love and faithfulness!"

Psalm 115:1 (NIV)

Trilogy Christian Publishers
A Wholly Owned Subsidiary of Trinity Broadcasting Network
2442 Michelle Drive
Tustin, CA 92780

For information, address Trilogy Christian Publishing

Rights Department, 2442 Michelle Drive, Tustin, Ca 92780.

Trilogy Christian Publishing/ TBN and colophon are trademarks of Trinity Broadcasting Network.

For information about special discounts for bulk purchases, please contact Trilogy Christian Publishing.

Manufactured in the United States of America

Trilogy Disclaimer: The views and content expressed in this book are those of the author and may not necessarily reflect the views and doctrine of Trilogy Christian Publishing or the Trinity Broadcasting Network.

10 9 8 7 6 5 4 3 2 1

Library of Congress Cataloging-in-Publication Data is available.

ISBN 978-1-68556-785-9
ISBN 978-1-68556-786-6 (ebook)

Dedication

To the joy, strength, and inspiration of family:

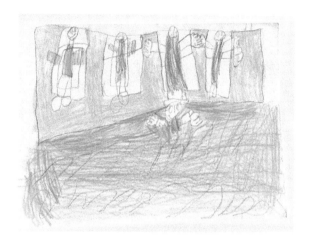

"Who's that in the water?" I asked my younger grandson, who had drawn this picture of their family foursome plus one. "That's you, Gram," he replied proudly.

Drenched in our Creator's Son-shine, may we always live out God's best for us, recognizing and sharing His blessings.

"Love one another as I have loved you" (John 13:34).

Table of Contents

1 - "Rejoice in the Lord always. Again, I say Rejoice!" Phil. 4:4 (NIV)

Restored

Winterset

A New Spirit

Espiritu

Seal of Faith

God is Light

At the House of Plenty

The Invitation

2 - "Let your gentleness be evident to all." Phil. 4:5a (NIV)

His Eye is on the Sparrow

Her War

The Way

Souljourn

Oh Pharisaical Me

Fill Me, Lord

3 - "The Lord is near." Phil. 4:5b (NIV)

At the Well

When I Met You

At His Holy Hill

Veritas

As One with the Father

To My Loved Ones

Defender of our Souls

4 - "Do not be anxious about anything, but in everything, by prayer and petition, with thanksgiving, present your requests to God." Phil. 4:6 (NIV)

Prayer of Psalm 56
Psalm 18: The Lord is My Rock
Drowning Cry for Help
Out of the Depths I Cry to You, Lord
Ezekial 17:24
Worry
Endless Night
On the Banks of the Jabbok
Futility of Worry

5 - "And the peace of God, which transcends all understanding, will guard your hearts and minds in Christ Jesus." Phil. 4:7 (NIV)

The Shadow
Surrender
My Prayer
Refining Reliance
Star-Portal
Exalted

6 - "Whatever is true, noble, right, pure, lovely, admirable— if anything is excellent or praiseworthy, think about such things." Phil. 4:8 (NIV)

The Journey
Sunset
February Night
Rainbow Covenant
Teach Me, Lord
Finale

1

**"Rejoice in the Lord always.
Again, I say Rejoice:"**

Phil. 4:4 (NIV)

Restored

"This [sister] of yours was dead and is alive again;
was lost and is found."*

It was not You who drifted away, but I—
pointing my finger in every direction
except that of truth,
driving a wedge decades-wide between
Your heart and mine,
stunting the growth of our relationship,
always believing—at some level—in our eventual reunion;
yet I tended our garden
with neglect.

You called my wandering heart
again and again
(I see that now, looking back)
but I did not hear or
chose not to listen.

Then a gust of grace blew open the door I thought I'd closed;
the light of Your love streamed in, startling my soul.

At last I've found You
right here
where I left You.

*Luke 15:24 (NIV)

WINTERSET

"Here I am! I stand at the door and knock.
If anyone hears my voice and opens the door,
I will come in and eat with that person, and they
with me."*

It was late winter in my soul
when first He came knocking.
My door was latched tight against the cold.

He rapped softly—like a question.
I hesitated, vacillated.
He knocked again, insistently.

Opening cautiously, only a crack,
I was greeted by a rush of spring scented
with freedom:

"It is for freedom that Christ has set us free."**

*Rev. 3:20; **Gal. 5:1b (NIV)

A New Spirit

My soul stirs at the
tender orchestration
of new morning music
flowing from the depth of Your Love,
blending in perfect harmony with the
pulsing rhythm of a heartbeat—
enveloping music, softly sighing,
creating a new spirit within me.

"I will give you a new heart
and put a new spirit in you;
I will remove from you your heart of stone
and give you a heart of flesh.
I will put my Spirit in you
and move you to follow my decrees...
you will be my people
and I will be your God."*

*Ezekiel 36:26-28 (NIV)

Espiritu

"The Spirit of God has made me;
the breath of the Almighty
gives me life."*

My God, my God,
You set me free—
adrift on the breath
of Your Spirit!

"…the Spirit gives birth to spirit….
The wind blows where it pleases.
You hear its sound
but you cannot tell where it comes from
or where it is going.
So it is with everyone born of the Spirit."**

Let the winds of Your will
fill the sails of my soul;
chart my course
home
to Your harbor.

*Job 33:4 (NIV)
**John 3:6-8 (NIV)

SEAL OF FAITH

I remember the day,
the moment
You called my heart.
Moved by Your Spirit,
I answered;
You offered,
I accepted;
You promised,
I believed.

It was then I knew
You had
"set [Your] seal of ownership
upon me
and put [Your] Spirit in [my] Heart..."*

You planted faith in my soul,
and Your poetry took root.

*2 Cor. 1:22 (NIV)

GOD IS LIGHT

"…the darkness is passing
and the true light is already shining."*
It is the new morning of Truth,
the dawn of endless day;
it is the dusk – the final demise –
of deceit.

Children of the Light,
delight in hope;
The Son has risen!
Today we see
"The path of the righteous is
like the morning sun,
shining ever brighter
till the full light of day."**

*1 John 2:8b (NIV)
**Prov. 4:18 (NIV)

AT THE HOUSE OF PLENTY

"They feast on the abundance of Your house;
You give them drink from Your river of delights."*

When I feast on Your abundance
I find my spirit filled;
when I drink from Your sweet waters
my thirsty soul is stilled.

Lord, please fill me
—as a vessel—
with Your love, Your will, Your grace.
I'll find fullness at Your table
till I meet You
face to face.

*Ps. 36:8 (NIV)

The Invitation

"Blessed are those who are invited
to the wedding supper of the Lamb!"*

I received an invitation
to the Wedding of the Lamb.
I knew I was not worthy—
He said He'd take me as I am.

Though my wedding garb
was soiled
it's now been cleaned and pressed.
I accept His invitation;
my spirit has found rest.

*Rev. 19:9b (NIV)

2

"Let your gentleness be evident to all."

Phil. 4:5a (NIV)

His Eye is on the Sparrow – A True Story

"But not a single sparrow can fall to the ground
without your Father knowing it."*

Lying face down in the snow,
blood seeping from his nose,
nothing moves except
the widening stain of red
beneath his stubbled face.
Black knit cap askew,
Too-large brown wool coat
fans out on either side
in large, winged triangles;
he resembles a fallen bird with
the face of a man.
Passers-by go about their business.

Dad cannot;
he asks me to stop the car.

Nudging his brown, wooly back,
Dad summons him up from his stupor.
The sickeningly sweet odor of alcohol
mingles with blood, grime, and aging sweat.

(cont. on next page)

Wordlessly, Dad wipes his face and,
with an arm under each wing,
helps him to his feet;
together they wobble across the street
toward the clinic…

I wait outside.

Bloodstains darken on the snow;
the lesson is tattooed on my heart.

"But a Samaritan, as he traveled,
came where the man was, and when he saw him,
he took pity on him."**

*Matt 10:29b (NLT)
**Luke 10:33 (NIV)

HER WAR

Nothing moves
except the tears
crawling out of vacuous eyes,
coursing around the curves of her nose,
kissing the corners of her mouth
then plunging
from her chin
as though dropping off a cliff.

She wore her war
like a shroud.

Hours later
and a world away
I watch the full moon rise.
It wears her face.
Nothing moves except those tears.

"…my eyes pour out tears to God;
…plead with God
 as [one] pleads for his friend."*

                                        *Job 16:20-21 (NIV)

The Way

"Whether you turn to the right or to the left, your ears will hear a voice behind you saying, 'This is the way; walk in it.'"*

As far as my soul can see
this is the way of
truth and light,
the path that takes me home.

My soul lived in the mind of God
long before it was chambered
in this earthbound body.

From before time till after time,
my soul rests
in the stillness my Savior provides.

A peace pervades
despite breathless anticipation
in the knowledge of what awaits…

The only Way,
the whole Truth,
the essence of Life.

*Is. 30:21 (NIV)

SOULJOURN

"...Say to my soul, 'I am your salvation.'"*
Sometimes my soul speaks softly to its Maker
with a familiarity bred of long acquaintance
as though it had been introduced before time began
while the heart of me marvels and eavesdrops
on this affectionate exchange
between created and Creator.

Sometimes my soul cries out to its Maker
with an anguish born of pain, loss, confusion—
forgetting, for the moment, that the Comforter promises,
"My presence will go with you and I will give you rest." **

Sometimes my soul sings to its Maker;
spinning unbridled pirouettes,
it dances among the clouds
in the ageless choreography
of the song of its Creator.

Sometimes my soul is still,
resting in awe of its Maker;
my whole being pauses
to ponder this Prince of Peace
who knew my soul before I was.

*Ps. 35:3 (NIV)
**Ex. 33:14b (NIV)

OH, PHARISAICAL ME!

Bobbing in my bubble of
self-righteousness…

God's finger gently tapped the surface,
creating trembling, concentric circles,
disrupting my comfortable cocoon.

I heard my name as
He called my heart,
bringing hidden things to light:
Review
Remember
Repent

"…the Lord searches every heart and understands every
desire and every thought."*

*1 Chron. 28:9 (NIV)

Fill Me, Lord

"May the words of my mouth and the meditation
of my heart be pleasing in Your sight, O Lord, my
Rock and my Redeemer."*

Fill my eyes with You, O Lord,
that all between
my here and now
and the goal that is You
be aligned with Your will.

Fill my days with Your reflection
wrapping around each moment,
each thought,
each person I encounter,
each choice I make.

Fill my heart with Your song:
lifting, lilting,
layered song
of oneness with You.

Fill my life with contentment
in Your grace,
Your provision,
Your abundance.

(cont'd on next page)

Fill me with Your presence, Lord.
Let Your light and love overflow,
radiating Your promises,
flooding all in my path.

*Ps. 19:14 (NIV)

3

"The Lord is Near"

Phil. 4:5b (NIV)

At the Well

"Jesus answered, 'Everyone who drinks this water will be thirsty again, but whoever drinks the water I give will never thirst. The water I give will become in [you] a spring of water welling up to eternal life.'"*

"Will you give Me a drink?"
He asked,
tired from His journey,
thirsty,
but with no vessel to draw water.

She didn't recognize
that it was *she* who thirsted,
that it was *He* who offered
living water, and
that *He* was the vessel.

*John 4:13-14 (NIV)

WHEN I MET YOU, LORD...

a rainbow of light
penetrated my darkness;
my spirit uncoiled.

At His Holy Hill

Psalm 99

With my spirit soaring blissfully
on the wings of Your promises,
swooping,
spiraling
in the stillness beyond the clouds,
I suddenly,
unexpectedly
veer so close to Your feet
that I recoil—
stunned,
trembling at the sudden awareness of
Your breathtaking
Holiness!

"Exalt the Lord our God and worship at His footstool;
He is holy."*

*Ps 99:5 (NIV)

VERITAS

As the sun
gives light,
warmth,
direction,
defining day
and night,

without which
no hope of life,
only death…

so the Son.
So the Son!

As One with the Father

From behind the beveled glass
a single lightbulb peered
creating its own tiny rainbow
on the wall beside me.

The single light,
whole and white,
was transformed, multi-hued
as it softly pierced the glass
and whispered to me of
the Trinity.

One light,
one nature,
one...

To My Loved Ones
Who Do Not Yet Believe

"Ask and it will be given to you; seek and you will find, knock and the door will be opened to you."*

You stand on the shore
of an ocean of grace,
afraid to wade in,
afraid that you'll taste
the truth you're avoiding.

Like sand through your fingers—
the directions you've tried,
the groanings of spirit
and tears that you've cried;
yet you stand
empty-handed.

As wave after wave
washes steadily closer
you retreat to dry sand
glancing over your shoulder—
wondering, wistful, but wary.

*Matt. 7:7 (NIV)

DEFENDER OF OUR SOULS

Do you ever wonder what protected you
from harm that night?
You remember—
That night.

"What is man that You are mindful of him,
the son of man that You care for him?"*

Remember those times when, despite
wrong choices,
bad habits,
inattention...
God seemingly rewrote the script,
intervening, rescuing,
defending, deflecting,
dropping His armor over us?

"For You have delivered me from death
and my feet from stumbling
that I may walk before God in the light of life."**

(cont'd on next page)

Looking back at the unexplainables,
near misses,
frozen moments
wrongly labeled
luck, chance, fate...
I see You in my rearview mirror,
Loving Father, Friend,
Defender of my soul.

"...and what does the Lord require of [us]?
To act justly, to love mercy, and
to walk humbly with [our] God."***

*Ps. 8:4 (ESV)
**Ps. 56:13 (NIV)
***Micah 6:8b (NIV)

4

"Do not be anxious about anything, but in every situation, by prayer and petition, with thanksgiving, present your requests to God."

Phil. 4:6 (NIV)

Prayer of Psalm 56

"**P**ut my tears in Your bottle, Lord…

are they not recorded in your book?"*

Remind me now,

so that when I am

Afraid, I will put my trust in You,

You, and only You!

Every sorrow has been tallied,

every promise has been kept.

Remember the words of this psalm:

"… I can walk in Your presence, O God,
in Your life-giving light."**

*Ps. 56:8b (AMP)
**Ps. 56:13b (NLT)

PSALM 18

"The Lord is my Rock..."*

My strength was an illusion—
something I imagined in myself
while the mainstream directed my course.
But when I turned against the current
the river rushed over me.
Clawing at the silt,
trying to regain my balance,
I only dug deeper,
deeper,
into the mire.

"In my distress I cried to my God for help...**
He reached down from on high
and took hold of me;

He drew me out of deep waters...***

He brought me out into a spacious place;
He rescued me
because He delighted in me."****

*Ps. 18:2a; **18:6a;
***18:16; ****18:19 (NIV)

Drowning Cry for Help

Once, as a child,
I jumped from a board
too high into a pool
too deep and realized
too late that I had not taken a deep enough breath.
Struggling, straining, clawing against my persistent plunge,
I wondered whether I had
the strength
the ability
the air
the time
the reserve
the energy
the fortitude
the experience
to reach the surface.

It's like that tonight.
I swim in grief.

"…You saw my affliction and knew the anguish
of my soul."*

"In my alarm I said, 'I am cut off from Your sight!'
Yet You heard my cry for mercy when I called to
You for help."**

*Ps. 31:7b; ** 31:22 (NIV)

"Out of the Depths I Cry to You, Lord"*

Confusion contorts my sense of order,
wrinkling my days and nights,
building detours on my
half-finished path.
Groping in this darkness
I am mocked by nothingness; my ears roar
as though held to the mouth of an empty seashell.
I wait.

In Your time You will, I know,
light my path
direct my way.

I wait, relying on
Your promises,
Your plan,
Your love,
Your faithfulness.

"I wait for the Lord,
my whole being waits...
in His Word I put my hope."**

*Ps. 130:1; **130:5 (NIV)

Ezekial 17:24

"All the trees of the forest will know that I, the Lord, bring down the tall tree and make the low tree grow tall. I dry up the green tree and make the dry tree flourish."*

> Sometimes
> God calls my heart
> by first reducing me to
> a spiritual skeleton,
> allowing comfort trappings
> to *slip* from my grasp
> as easily as leaves from a tree
> after a hard frost.
>
> Like a willow in winter
> I stand
> cold, vulnerable, unadorned,
> clad in a somber cloud.
>
> Through the winter
> I await spring rains,
> anticipating new growth.

"Let us acknowledge the Lord; let us press on to acknowledge Him. As surely as the sun rises, He will appear; He will come to us like…the spring rains that water the earth." **

*Ezekial 17:24 (NIV)
**Hosea 6:3 (NIV)

WORRY...

...like a lump of cold clay
lays heavy in my hands;
a malignant obstacle to hope.
I examine it from every side
attempting to create *something* I can
recognize,
relate to,
reason with.
But the more I attend to it
the more it
gathers girth;
I can no longer carry it.
I turn my back
hoping to abandon it
but
    find
       it
          follows.
Its goal,
it would seem,
to consume me.

"How long must I wrestle with my thoughts?"*
But I trust in Your unfailing love."**

*Psalm 13:2a; **Ps. 13:5a (NIV)

Endless Night

Kaleidoscopically
night evolves
grotesquely turning, twisting, tumbling
through gnarly nightvisions.

Clawing for consciousness,
I struggle through the seemingly
endless
night
pulling the darkness over my head
like a pall,
craving the dawn.

"I wait for the Lord
more than watchmen wait for the morning,
more than watchmen wait for the morning."*

*Ps. 130:6 (NIV)

On the Banks of the Jabbok

As dawn breaks
I emerge from my struggle
to face the sunrise.
I am a new creation
but today I walk with
a limping spirit.

Struggling with God
on the banks of the Jabbok,
daybreak found Jacob with
a new name,
a new beginning,
limping away from the person he'd been.

"Jacob replied, 'I will not let You go
unless You bless me'"*
"…Then He blessed him there."**

I crave Your *Sonrise* blessing, Lord.

*Gen. 32:26b; **32:29b (NIV)

Futility of Worry

"Who of you by worrying can add a single hour
to your life? Since you cannot do this very little
thing, why do you worry about the rest?"*

    I carefully pressed and folded
    my worries.
    Tucking them carefully into my backpack,
    hoisting the load to my shoulders,
    I struggled with the weight-- then
    hauled the burden to His feet.

    Laying out my bundled worries,
    I felt relief.

    Why, then, did I stuff them back into the pack
    strap it on
    and walk away?

*Luke 12:25-26

5

"The peace of God, which transcends all understanding, will guard your hearts and minds in Christ Jesus."

Phil 4:7 (NIV)

The Shadow

Startled by a shadow,
I was surprised to find it was my own.
Looming larger than life
it lay behind me on the path
as though dragging me by my feet.
I tried to outrun it
but was unable.
I tried to chase it away
but was unable.
Attempting to trample it,
I learned we were connected at the soles.

Dark and foreboding it lay before me,
mocking my every move;
devoid of light
it remained
the very image of me.

And then—
then I hid in the shadow of His wings and
my shadow disappeared!

*"He who dwells in the shadow of the Most
High will rest in the shadow of the Almighty....
Under His wings you will find refuge."

Ps. 91:1; 91:4b (NIV)

Surrender

Surrender,

in the best and worst of times is easily

Undone,

unraveled; but

Reminders

of redeeming love and promises repeated

Return

us to His feet as He

Encourages us:

Nothing to fear,

He says; lay it all

Down,

He says;

Every

every,

every moment abide in My presence,

listen, hear, respond, obey,

Rest,

rest, rest in Me.

My Prayer

My prayer hung heavily
in that space
before my face.
Ever present;
I thought only of
My Prayer.

As I stared transfixed,
my prayer became a mirror;
my face filled the frame,
lined with needs,
fears—an accurate reflection of
My Prayer.

Gradually a light
shone through the glass, rendering my prayer
transparent.
Trembling with realization,
I watched my vanishing reflection
as You gently adjusted my focus,
corrected my nearsightedness.

By allowing me to see
Your purpose beyond it,
You answered
my prayer.

Refining Reliance

With a sigh and upturned hands,
it seems, at first,
painful
to relinquish control.
Transiently
there's an expanding void
as though I'm being poured out;
but just as quickly
I sense my spirit
anticipating
the inrush
of Your peace,
strength,
the warmth of Your love.

Trust is not finite.
I'm learning that.
Again and again
it must occur,
leaving that vacuum which awaits
the fullness of Your Spirit.

"When anxiety was great within me,
Your consolation brought me joy."*

*Ps. 94:19 (NIV)

STAR-PORTAL

Searching the night sky
horizon to horizon,
sorting the stars…
I seek the broadest,
the brightest.

Finding it,
hoping it could be
the portal,
I stare deeply
imagining
God
staring back.

"We fix our eyes not on what is seen,
 but on what is unseen, since
 what is seen is temporary,
 but what is unseen is eternal."*

*2 Cor. 4:18 (NIV)

EXALTED

"Be still and know that I am God; I will be exalted
among the nations. I will be exalted in the earth."*

Be still.
Clear of clutter,
concern,
conversation,
come into His presence.
Be still,
quiet,
motionless,
receptive as the night
in its final breath before dawn.
Be still,
peace-filled,
rising above earth's tether,
floating heavenward
soundlessly, effortlessly.
"Be still and know that
I am God."
Be still...
alert to the whisper of His voice
"...***know that***
I
Am
GOD."

*Ps. 46:10 (NIV)

6

"Whatever is true, noble, right, pure, lovely, admirable—if anything is excellent or praiseworthy—think about such things."

Phil. 4:8 (NIV)

The Journey

Lost in doubt through introspection,
seeking answers in His Word
I found promise and direction.

Moved to *faith* by His design
I ventured forth, though still uncertain,
taking one step at a time.

Finding *hope* in His endurance,
I saw light at every turn
as I leaned on His assurance.

Wrapped in *love* beyond dimension
I embrace His Way and Truth.
Joy exceeds all comprehension!

SUNSET

"The heavens declare the glory of God; the skies proclaim the work of His hands."*

A visual symphony,
this sunset
that wears but
a few bars
of the hues
of Your grandeur
like a fragment of
the hem
of Your glory.
All else becomes monochromatic
in the shadow of
this
holy manna for the eyes.

*Ps. 19:1(NIV)

February Night

"…I consider Your heavens,
 the work of Your fingers…"*

A holy breathing presence
pervades this star-littered night
with rhythmic expirations alternately
misting,
clearing,
leaving a vacuum of icy black
and absent moon

while the steady steely silence of
inspiration
leans solidly,
claiming
space.

*Ps. 8:3a (NIV)

Rainbow Covenant of *Genesis 9:12-17*

Suddenly a rainbow appeared,
a transparent overlay
on the dusky face
of the mountain,
arching high into the heavens,
streaming back to earth
from behind the storm clouds.

The setting sun witnessed the scene
and for a moment
ceased its descent.

"Whenever the rainbow appears in the clouds
I will see it
and remember the everlasting covenant
between God and all living creatures
*of every kind on the earth."**

His covenant spans the generations—
a spiritual rainbow
embracing His creation.

*Gen. 9:16 (NIV)

Teach Me, Lord

As this day ends
I wonder, Lord:
    did I live out
        Your will for me today?
It seemed an ordinary day—
a little sun,
a little rain
as I moved from
task to task.
    Were my words
        Your words?
    Did my footsteps
        follow Yours?
    Was I a reflection of Your light?

Or might I have overlooked
You
in the souls I encountered today?

"Teach us to number our days
That we may gain a heart of wisdom."*

Ps. 90:12 (NIV)

Finale

Pain and sadness
groaning of hearts,
anguished spirits
and worlds torn apart—
soothed and healed
by Your perfect will;
from living waters
souls take their fill.

Turn this world
toward Your shining face;
shape our hearts
and rain down Your grace;
call, O Shepherd,
Your wandering souls;
light their way
back into Your fold.

You wash our souls
with the blood of Your love—
garnered salvation,
gift of Your Son.

(cont. on next page)

Mindful of promises
though worthy of none,
we're saved by Your grace;
now victory's won.

Blow Your trumpet
calling us home,
raise the valleys
and lay mountains low;
day of judgment,
Scripture fulfilled,
New Jerusalem!—

Souls finally stilled.

EPILOGUE

"Whatever you have learned or received
or heard or seen in [this]—put it into practice.
And the God of peace will be with you."

Phil 4:9 (NIV)

"Rejoice in the Lord always,
I will say it again: Rejoice!"

Phil. 4:4 (NIV)

ABOUT THE AUTHOR

Kathleen Claussen artistically weaves poetic word-art from life's peaks, valleys, and deserts, while intertwining Scripture passages that inspire, enhance, color, and complete the lines.

From a smalltown midwestern start, to setting down roots in the four corner states, Kathleen has counterbalanced four decades in nursing careers with porch poems under the stars; family times rhythmically rocking babies; houseboat vacations; backpacking in the Rocky Mountains; desert hikes under impossibly blue skies; exhilarating hours on waterskis; quiet hammock siestas lulled by birdsong from swaying trees; and long bike rides with verses seemingly spinning out of the spokes.

Leaning on her faith in God and His Word for inspiration, clarity, application, and lift, Kathleen finds poetry to be as essential to the soul as respiration. It expresses life in its most basic dimensions even when life – true to form – becomes riddled with potholes, twists and turns, cumbersome peaks, and dry deserts, the final tapestry is still signed and hung in full view.

Printed in the USA
CPSIA information can be obtained
at www.ICGtesting.com
JSHW071532100823
46228JS00009B/40